AUTHOR'S HILL PRESENTS

THE WORST THING EVER HAPPENED

Find it with "ISBN"

जय श्री कृष्णा

Jatin bharat

(FOUNDER OF "AUTHOR'S HILL")

AUTHOR'S HILL

"Author's Hill" Is A Club Of Passionate Writers Dedicated To Creativity, Authenticity, And Empowerment Through The Written Word. United By A Commitment To Genuine Storytelling, We Strive To Inspire Change And Evoke Deep Emotions Through Our Diverse Narratives. Each Member Brings A Unique Perspective, Contributing To A Rich Tapestry Of Literary Voices That Celebrate Individuality And Collective Growth. We Are Advocates For Lifelong Learning, Collaboration, And The Power Of Expression, Continually Honing Our Craft To Reflect The Dynamic World Around Us. Join Us In This Journey Of Discovery, As We Explore The Boundless Possibilities Of Writing And Imagination.

THE WORST THING EVER HAPPENED

In "The Worst Thing Ever Happened," A
Collection Of Heartfelt And Poignant Stories,
Multiple Authors Come Together To Share The
Most Harrowing Experiences Of Their Lives.
This Book Dives Deep Into Personal Tragedies
And Trials, Revealing The Raw, Unfiltered
Emotions That Accompany Life's Darkest
Moments. Each Narrative Offers A Unique
Perspective On Pain And Resilience, Making It A
Profound Exploration Of The Human Spirit's
Ability To Endure And Overcome The
Unimaginable. Through These Compelling Stories,
Readers Are Invited To Reflect On
Their Own Experiences And Find Solace In The
Shared Journey Of Suffering And Hope.

A Message to Respected Anurag Anand

Your generosity knows no bounds, much like our friendship that flourished without ever meeting in person. As an IITian from IIT Kharagpur, you chose to support a stranger's dream, enabling this book's publication when various hurdles stood in the way.

Anurag bhai, your belief in our work, formed solely through our digital interactions, not only made this book possible but also taught me the true meaning of trust and kindness. Your support has left an indelible mark on our journey as an author.

Thank you for proving that distance is no barrier to making a profound difference in someone's life.

Preface

Life's Darkest Moments
Often Test Our Limits And Reveal Our Deepest
Strengths. "The Worst Thing Ever Happened" Is
A Collection Of Stories Where Individuals Share
Their Most Harrowing Experiences, Shedding
Light On The Profound Resilience And Enduring
Hope That
Reside Within Us All.
Each Narrative In This Anthology Invites You
Into A Deeply Personal Journey Through Pain
And Adversity. These Stories Not Only
Highlight The Raw And Unfiltered Emotions That
Accompany Life's Greatest Challenges But Also
Offer A Testament To The Indomitable Spirit
That Carries Us Through. As You Read, May
You Find Empathy, Strength, And A Renewed
Appreciation For The Power Of Human
Connection And Resilience.
We Hope These Accounts Provide Solace And
Inspiration, Reminding You
That Even In Our Darkest Hours,
We Are Never Truly Alone.

Aknowledgment

"I extend my sincere gratitude to the entire Notion press team for their exceptional support throughout our publishing journey. Your expertise and guidance have been instrumental in bringing this book to life.

We owe a profound debt of gratitude to Devraj Kousik for his outstanding assistance and unwavering support. Your contributions have been truly invaluable to this book.

My co-author, Bornali Ray, is especially thankful to Notion press for this remarkable opportunity. She expresses her deepest appreciation for the platform to share her story with the world.

We also want to acknowledge Haidar and Sachin, participants who generously shared their stories for our book, enriching its content and impact.

Thank you, Notion press, for being an integral part of our literary journey

CONTENT

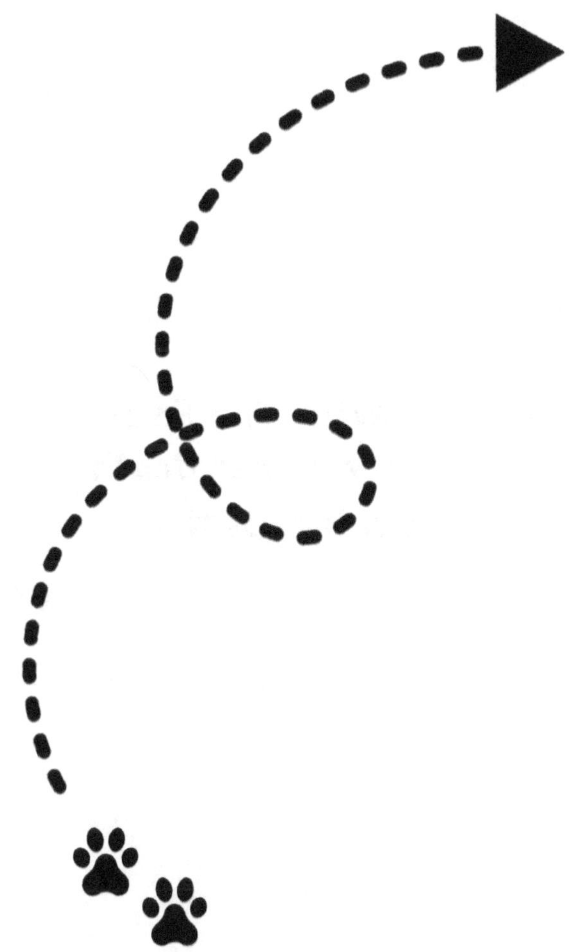

(She Left Me With The Empty Hands)
...a story of her death
(Sachin Seth)

See Left Me With The Empty Hands
(a story of her death)

The Tapestry of Love

In the vast tapestry of life, love shines like a constellation of stars, guiding us through the darkest nights. It's an invisible force, weaving threads of affection and warmth between hearts, drawing souls together in a dance as old as time itself. Everyone yearns for this profound connection, this sense of belonging. Some are fortunate enough to find it, basking in its glow. Others, like me, experience its radiance only to have it cruelly snatched away by the capricious hands of fate.

Love is a universal language, spoken in whispers and shouts, in gentle touches and passionate embraces. It's the force that moves mountains and calms storms, that inspires great works of art and small acts of kindness. In my journey, I've come to understand that love is not just a feeling, but a living, breathing entity that shapes our very existence.

As I reflect on my own story, I'm reminded of the countless ways love manifests itself in our lives. It's in the laughter shared between friends, the comforting embrace of family, and the heart-stopping moment when you first lock eyes with your soulmate. Love is the thread that binds us all, connecting us across time and space in ways we may never fully comprehend.

A Fateful Encounter

My story begins in the hallowed halls of a college, where the pursuit of knowledge served as a backdrop to a far more profound quest - the search for love. We were students, our noses often buried in textbooks, but our eyes had a will of their own. They would wander, seeking each other out across crowded lecture halls and quiet library corners. These fleeting glances were like whispered secrets between our hearts, each look a promise, a question, an answer.

I remember the first time I saw her, standing in the sunlight streaming through the library windows. Her hair caught the light, creating a halo effect that made her seem almost ethereal. She was engrossed in a book, her brow furrowed in concentration, and I found myself captivated by the intensity of her focus. In that moment, I knew my life had changed irrevocably.

The day we finally met felt predestined, as if every moment of our lives had been leading us to this intersection of fate. Time seemed to slow as we talked, our words flowing effortlessly, punctuated by shy smiles and nervous laughter. We discovered shared passions for literature and philosophy, debating the merits of different authors and theories late into the night. From that day forward, we spent every possible moment together, weaving our lives into a beautiful tapestry of shared dreams and unbridled happiness.

The Blossoming of Love

Our joy was like the first warm rays of sun after a long, cold winter - it seeped into our bones, thawing the loneliness we hadn't even realized was there. Even now, years later, I can close my eyes and almost feel the warmth of her hand in mine, her fingers intertwined with my own as if they were always meant to be there.

As the days turned into weeks and months, our love blossomed like a rare and beautiful flower. We studied together, poring over textbooks late into the night, our academic pursuits intertwined with stolen kisses and whispered words of encouragement. We shared our deepest secrets, our hopes and fears, laying bare our souls to each other.

Together, we explored the world around us, finding wonder in the simplest things - a sunset painted across the sky, the melody of rainfall on a tin roof, the comforting aroma of chai on a chilly morning. We would spend hours in the local park, lying on the grass and pointing out shapes in the clouds. Every moment was an adventure, every conversation a journey of discovery.

Our love grew stronger with each passing day, nurtured by shared experiences and mutual understanding. We supported each other through exam stress and family conflicts, celebrating each other's successes and providing comfort in times of failure. It was during this time that I truly understood the meaning of the phrase "two halves of a whole."

Shadows on the Horizon

When we were together, I felt invincible, as if I had unlocked the secrets of the universe. My love was by my side, my family supported our relationship, and the future stretched out before us like an endless road of possibilities. We made grand plans for our future - the careers we would pursue, the places we would travel, the home we would build together. The world was our oyster, and we were determined to find every pearl.

But life, in its infinite wisdom and cruelty, had other plans. Our story was about to take an unexpected turn, one that would test the very foundations of our love. As time passed, I began to sense a shift, a subtle change in the air around us. Even though she remained the centre of my universe, a nagging worry began to gnaw at the edges of my consciousness.

Our joy, once pure and unbridled, became tinged with an undercurrent of fear and uncertainty. On rainy days, I would imagine her twirling in the droplets, her laughter echoing in my mind, a bittersweet reminder of happier times. She began to withdraw, her smiles becoming less frequent, her eyes clouded with a sadness I couldn't understand.

I tried to reach out, to bridge the growing gap between us, but it felt like trying to catch smoke with my bare hands.

The Battle for Love

Together, we weathered countless challenges, including the disapproval of family members who couldn't understand the depth of our connection. Her parents, traditional in their outlook, were hesitant about our relationship. They worried about our different backgrounds and the impact it might have on her future. My family, while more accepting, had their own reservations.

But we fought for our love, enduring hardships with unwavering determination. We stood firm in our commitment to each other, facing each obstacle as a united front. We had long conversations with our families, explaining our feelings and our plans for the future. Slowly, gradually, we began to win them over. They saw the strength of our bond, the positive influence we had on each other, and finally, our families saw the truth of our bond and gave us their blessing.

Despite the official approval of our families, there was still a thrill in our secret meetings. We would sneak away to quiet corners of the campus, sharing private moments away from prying eyes. Her eyes, deep and soulful, were like twin pools of midnight sky, twinkling with starlight. I could lose myself in those eyes for hours, always finding my way back to her. Every touch, every shared glance, was a silent promise of a future filled with love and laughter.

The Cruel Twist of Fate

But even as we reveled in our joy, shadows began to creep into our world. She spoke often of a pain, a hurt that I, in my blissful state, failed to fully comprehend. At first, it was just occasional complaints of fatigue or headaches. I dismissed them as stress from our studies or perhaps the emotional toll of our earlier struggles. I was too consumed by my own happiness, too blinded by the brilliance of our love to see the storm clouds gathering on the horizon. It's a failure that will haunt me for the rest of my days, a cruel reminder of how self-absorbed I had become.

One day, she told me she needed to visit a relative for a few days. The thought of being apart was painful, but I supported her decision, believing it would be just a short separation. Days stretched into weeks, and her absence became a gaping void in my life. Our daily calls became less frequent, her messages shorter and more cryptic. I reached out to her friends, desperate for any news, but they were as much in the dark as I was.

Fear began to take root in my heart, growing with each passing day. I couldn't shake the feeling that something was terribly wrong. Then, like a bolt from the blue, I learned the truth she had been hiding - a severe illness that had taken her to the hospital. The news hit me like a physical blow, shattering the perfect world we had built together.

The Last Goodbye

I rushed to the hospital, my heart pounding with a mixture of fear and desperate hope. I found her lying in a sterile hospital bed, looking fragile and vulnerable. The sight of her, pale and weakened, was almost more than I could bear. I brought her favourite fruits, a pitiful offering in the face of her suffering. As I sat by her side, holding her hand, I felt as though I was being torn apart from the inside. But I forced a smile, trying to be strong for her sake. I spoke of our future plans, of the life we would build together, anything to bring that beautiful smile back to her face. And when she did smile, even in her weakened state, it was like a ray of sunshine breaking through storm clouds, a reminder of the love that still bound us together.

I didn't know then how critical her condition was, that an operation loomed on the horizon. Our last meeting was a blur of words left unsaid and promises we both knew might never be kept. We talked about trivial things, avoiding the elephant in the room, both of us pretending that this was just a temporary setback. As I left that day, I turned back at the door for one last look. She blew me a kiss, her eyes filled with a love and sadness that will stay with me forever.

Two days later, I received a call that she wanted to see me. Hope surged in my heart, and I rushed to the hospital, my mind filled with thoughts of reunion and recovery. I imagined walking into her room to find her sitting up,

perhaps reading a book, ready to come home and continue our life together.

But when I arrived, the scene that greeted me was one of mourning. The room was heavy with grief, and from across the crowded space, I saw her lifeless form. In that moment, my world collapsed. I cried like a child, my sorrow a tidal wave that threatened to drown me. She was gone, and with her, she took all my hopes, all my dreams, and the future we had so carefully planned together.

The Long Night of the Soul

Her death left me adrift, a lost soul in a world that suddenly seemed devoid of color and meaning. The pain was unbearable, a constant, gnawing ache that consumed my every waking moment. I couldn't bear to stay in the city where every street corner, every café, every classroom held memories of her. I fled to Mumbai, seeking anonymity in the bustling city, hoping to lose myself in its chaos.

For three long years, I wandered the streets of Mumbai like a ghost, a shadow of my former self. I drowned my sorrows in alcohol and drugs, desperately trying to numb the pain that consumed me. Nights blurred into days in a haze of substance-induced oblivion. I lost touch with my family, my friends, and myself. The person I had been, the man she had loved, seemed like a distant memory, a character in a story I had once read.

In my darkest moments, I made several attempts to end my life, longing to join her in whatever lay beyond this mortal coil. But fate, it seemed, had other plans. Each time, something or someone intervened - a concerned stranger, a moment of clarity, a fleeting memory of her smile that made me hesitate just long enough. I survived, though I knew not why, and slowly, painfully, I began to realize that I had to live - if not for myself, then for those who still loved me, and for her memory.

Finding Solace

It was during one of these dark nights, lost in a haze of alcohol and regret, that I stumbled upon a small bookstore tucked away in a quiet corner of the city. The old wooden sign creaked as I pushed open the door, and the smell of aged paper and ink enveloped me like a comforting embrace. The owner, an elderly man with kind eyes, looked up from behind the counter and offered me a sympathetic smile. "Lost souls often find solace among these shelves," he said softly, his voice tinged with wisdom born of years spent surrounded by stories.

As I wandered through the store, I began to think about my partner, whose life had been tragically cut short by severe kidney stones. The pain of her loss had left a void that seemed impossible to fill, but the quiet serenity of the bookstore provided a temporary respite from my grief. The bookstore owner, who became a friend and mentor, encouraged me to channel my emotions into something constructive. At first, it was just fragments of memories and scattered thoughts. But as time passed, I found comfort in talking about her, sharing our story with others, and keeping her memory alive through the stories I told.

Rediscovering Life's Color

Talking about our experiences became my way of coping, a method to confront my grief and explore the depths of my emotions without fear. Each conversation felt like a step on the path to healing. I relived our happiest moments and confronted my deepest regrets. Through these memories, I found a way to keep her spirit alive, to honor the love we had shared.

As the years passed, life slowly began to regain its color. The ache in my heart softened, replaced by a bittersweet gratitude for having loved so deeply and passionately. I found solace in the belief that her spirit lived on in the hearts of those who had known and cherished her, and that our love, though tested by tragedy, had left an indelible mark on the tapestry of eternity.

I began to see glimpses of her in the world around me - in the laughter of children playing in the park, in the kindness of strangers, in the beauty of a sunset. These moments, once painful reminders of what I had lost, became cherished connections to her memory. I realized that by living fully, by embracing life with the same passion and joy she had shown, I could honor her in the most meaningful way possible.

An Eternal Echo

Now, as I write these final words, I am reminded of the profound truth that love, in all its forms, is the essence of our existence. It transcends the boundaries of time and space, weaving us together in an intricate web of shared experiences and enduring connections. Her love continues to inspire me, guiding me towards a future where her memory is not a source of pain, but a beacon of hope and a reminder to cherish each moment as a precious gift.

This, then, is not merely a story of a love lost, but of a love that endures beyond the confines of mortality - a testament to the power of love to transcend life and death, and to the resilience of the human spirit in the face of unimaginable loss. In the end, it is love that defines us, that shapes our journey through this life and beyond, connecting us all in ways we may never fully understand but will always deeply feel.

As I close this chapter of my life, I do so with a heart full of love - for her, for the journey we shared, and for the person I have become through this experience. Our story, like all great love stories, does not end with separation or death. It lives on, an eternal echo resonating through time, a reminder that true love is indeed boundless and eternal.

(Maybe I'll Die Soon)
(Jatin Bharat)

Maybe I'll Die Soon

Six Months in Prayagraj: A New Beginning

I had been in Prayagraj for about six months, living near a beautiful *Ganga* ghat and several stunning temples. My new home wasn't just conveniently located; it was spiritually uplifting. I planned to visit the ghat every day and worship at the temples once I settled in fully. The spiritual atmosphere filled me with hope for the future, making me believe that my life would take a wonderful new direction.

Every morning, the sound of bells from the nearby temples served as my natural alarm clock. The chanting of mantras and the *Ganga aarti*, which I could witness from my home, created a sense of peace and inspiration. This setting made me feel connected to something bigger, giving me the energy and optimism to start each day with a positive outlook.

I often took long walks along the ghats, absorbing the calmness of the flowing river and the devotion of the people around me. The sacredness of the place seemed to wash away my worries, leaving me with a deep sense of contentment. I felt that this new chapter in Prayagraj was just the beginning of a journey filled with growth, understanding, and fulfillment.

April 29th: A Day of Hope and Unexpected Turns

It was April 29th, a day that began with bright promise and the refreshing touch of a light rain. My friend and I started our morning with a comforting breakfast of chole chawal (chickpeas and rice). Though we had only been visiting the nearby library for two days, we were eager to immerse ourselves in our studies.

As we prepared to leave, I shared my excitement with my beloved over the phone. I painted a vivid picture of the enchanting temples, the mesmerizing Ganga aarti, and the morning bells that had become a delightful part of my routine. I told her how the temple bells, ringing out at dawn, gently woke me, filling me with peace and energy for the day ahead. The mantras chanted in the temples added a spiritual rhythm to my mornings, setting a perfect tone for the day.

Her happiness mirrored mine, as our lives were deeply connected. Knowing that these moments brought me joy made her just as content.

Reflecting on April 29th, I realized it was a day of hope and the beauty of life's surprises. The connection with my beloved, the excitement of new beginnings, and the delight in unexpected moments made it a day to remember. It was a reminder that while we can look forward to the future, the real magic lies in embracing the unplanned twists along the way.

The Library Visit and a Sudden Health Crisis

At the library, around two o'clock in the afternoon, I began to feel a pang of hunger. Deciding to take a brief break, I ventured to a nearby shop for some refreshments. I vividly recall drinking a refreshing mango shake and enjoying a bowl of mixed fruits. Satisfied, I returned to the library, eager to dive back into my studies.

As I settled into my chair, ready to resume my work, a faint pain started in my chest. I dismissed it as a minor, fleeting discomfort and continued studying. However, the situation quickly took a turn for the worse. Suddenly, I began coughing violently, and with each cough, a strange, liquid-like substance began to pour from my mouth. The library, being a Cyber Library, was dimly lit, and in the shadows, I initially thought it might be remnants of the juice I had drunk earlier.

Still believing it was just the juice, I rose to wash my hands and mouth, making my way towards the washroom. But with each step I took, the liquid flow from my mouth increased alarmingly. Panic set in as the substance seemed endless, gushing out uncontrollably.

Finally, as I reached the brighter area outside the library, the horrific reality struck me. In the light, I saw that it wasn't juice at all—it was blood, flowing continuously from my mouth, turning the mundane scene into a nightmare. The sight of the blood, vivid and terrifying, filled me with dread, and the gravity of the situation hit me with full force.

Emergency at the Hospital: Confusion and Concern

As the horrifying reality dawned on me that I was vomiting blood, my hands stained with my own life essence, my mind went blank with shock and fear.

Thousands of thoughts raced through my mind, leaving me stunned and deeply distressed in both body and soul. Amidst this turmoil, my friend, a police officer, swiftly took charge and rushed me to the nearby hospital.

During the short journey, blood continued to pour out in alarming quantities, a stark and terrifying reminder of the fragility of life. Arriving at the hospital, the doctors bombarded me with questions, trying to make sense of what had happened. Their responses varied wildly, adding to my confusion and anxiety.

One doctor, after a lengthy conversation, spoke of an energy within me that would lead me to great heights. Another, through gestures and expressions, hinted at the possibility of a grave illness like lung cancer. Each possibility weighed heavily on me, intensifying the turmoil within as I struggled to comprehend the suddenness and severity of my condition.

Just earlier that day, I had spoken with my beloved about our bright future, filled with hope and anticipation. Now, facing the stark contrast between those optimistic dreams and the grim possibilities presented by the doctors, I was overwhelmed by fear and uncertainty. The possibility of a serious illness or even death loomed large, casting a shadow over everything I had held dear.

Returning Home: A Night of Uncertainty

After some initial treatment and medicines, I was sent home to rest. The doctors had taken a blood sample, with the report due on Monday. My phone had been left at the library in the rush, so I used my friend's phone to call my sister. I explained the situation to her, trying to remain calm. She responded calmly, suggesting it might be a throat injury from coughing, but I could sense she was taking it very seriously. She immediately booked a train ticket for me to Kanpur for the next morning. When informing our mother, she downplayed the severity, saying only that my health had worsened and I needed to come home.

I returned to the library to collect my things and my phone. As soon as I got my phone, I called my beloved and told her about the entire incident, trying to present it in an interesting way despite its seriousness. She was stunned and scolded me, saying I had been negligent about my persistent cough. I remember her words were filled with extreme love, and she was crying a lot. She didn't want to trouble me by talking too much, knowing that speaking caused me to cough, which in turn brought more blood.

That night, I went out to drink pomegranate juice before trying to sleep, but sleep eluded me. I kept seeing my blood-soaked hands again and again in my mind. I felt as if my body was filled with blood from inside, which would come out if I spoke a little loudly and would completely decorate

me with red color again. The fear and uncertainty of what was happening to me made it impossible to rest peacefully.

The Journey Back to Kanpur: A Challenging Train Ride

I woke up at 5 am for an early morning train. Before leaving, I completely organized my room, holding onto the hope that I would return after a week of treatment. I went to the roof of my house for one last look around. I gazed towards the banks of the Ganga, the temples, and all the devotees who had come there. I observed the animals and the birds circling the temple, which seemed as if they too were worshipping. The sky was covered with black clouds, and I couldn't see it at all, unsure of what signal it was giving me. As I stood there, I felt drops of rain in my eyes, which would have been the most beautiful event of that day, but the emptiness inside me made me feel

extremely inauspicious. The incident of the
previous day was squeezing me from within.

My friend offered to accompany me to the
station, but after walking for a while, I
told him to let me go alone. I started
moving towards the railway station, towards
myself. On the way, I saw all the familiar sights
from the past six months. I felt I would come
back, but there was a voice inside that kept saying
this was the end. At the station, while waiting for
my train, I remembered the day I first came to
Prayagraj. The main difference was

that when I arrived, I was completely healthy,
both physically and mentally. Now, returning, I
looked as if someone had sucked the life out of me.

A loud train horn brought me back to reality. I
boarded what I thought was my train, only to
realize later it was the wrong one. My actual train
was running 2 hours late. Despite this mix-up, I
decided to continue on this train as it had already
come quite far. I spent half the journey standing
and half sitting in half a seat, which was harmful to
my health, but I managed to reach Kanpur safely.

Arrival in Kanpur: Facing Family and Friends

My house was near the station in Kanpur, so I knew everyone there. I couldn't meet anyone's eyes because my appearance had changed dramatically - my eyes had sunk in, my face had turned black, and every bone in my body was clearly visible. People looked at me with concern, asking what had happened and if my health was okay. I simply replied that my health had been a bit worse, which is why I had to come back.

When I reached home, everyone immediately understood the severity of my condition just by looking at me. Although no one in the house initially knew about the blood vomiting, my mom was very angry, believing I had been living carelessly in Prayagraj. They were surprised by my sudden return, as everything had seemed fine during our last conversation just yesterday morning.

By nightfall, another coughing fit revealed the truth about my condition to my family. My sister had also come from her in-laws' house to help.

Medical Consultations: Facing the Possibility of Lung Cancer

On May 1st, accompanied by my sister, I sat in Dr. Shetty's office, seeking answers amidst a storm of uncertainty. As I recounted the recent events that had brought me here, Dr. Shetty's expression grew serious. He gently mentioned the unsettling possibility: lung cancer.

In that moment, the world seemed to blur. Colors faded, leaving behind a haze of disbelief and fear. Despite the brightness of the room, I felt surrounded by darkness, grappling with the weight of Dr. Shetty's words.

To investigate further, Dr. Shetty ordered blood tests and X-rays, essential steps in understanding what was happening inside my body. Alongside, he administered an injection, explaining that any redness around the injection site could indicate issues in my lungs. Each test felt like a step into the unknown, where hope and worry intertwined.

As I left the hospital that day, the air felt heavier, each breath a reminder of the uncertainty ahead. Thoughts of my future with my beloved, once filled with dreams and plans, now mingled with the stark reality of potential illness. The contrast was stark and unsettling, yet amidst the fear, a glimmer of determination flickered—a resolve to face whatever lay ahead with courage and resilience.

Tests and More Tests: Seeking Answers

As the day approached for the test results, I noticed the injection site on my hand turning red—a troubling sign pointing to potential issues in my lungs. When the blood test and X-ray reports returned, they confirmed my worst fears: there were indeed significant problems with my lungs. Armed with these reports, we hurried back to Dr. Shetty the next day.
Dr. Shetty's demeanor turned grave as he reviewed the findings. He emphasized the seriousness of the situation and urgently referred us to Dr. Rajeev Kakkad, a renowned lung specialist.

The urgency was palpable; the constant presence of blood with every cough had become a grim reality, demanding immediate attention and treatment.

Upon meeting Dr. Rajeev Kakkad, he wasted no time in ordering a battery of tests, including a cancer screening scheduled for the following day. Other tests revealed swollen veins in my respiratory tract, alongside a sizable portion of my chest affected by bacterial infection.

Each test brought a mix of anxiety and hope—a desperate search for answers amidst mounting concerns about my health. The journey ahead seemed daunting, yet I clung to the possibility of finding clarity and a path towards recovery in the expertise of Dr. Kakkad and his team.

Dr. Rajeev Kakkad's Diagnosis: A Nine-Month Treatment Plan

Upon meeting Dr. Rajeev Kakkad, the gravity of my situation became starkly clear. He explained solemnly that for the next nine months, I would be unable to travel to any other city. Daily medication would be essential during this period, a regimen that shattered my hopes of returning to Prayagraj within a week. The house I had lovingly decorated and the life I had envisioned there suddenly closed off to me. The echoes of temple bells and the morning birdsong, once my anticipated daily companions, fell silent in an instant.

Dr. Kakkad prescribed potent medications to manage the recurring blood in my cough, which proved remarkably effective. Yet, he cautioned that any vigorous coughing could still trigger bleeding, reminding me of the precariousness of my condition.

The medications offered relief but also served as a constant reminder of the fragility of my health and the newfound limitations on my life. As I adjusted to this new reality, I clung to the hope that these treatments would pave the way for recovery and a return to the life I cherished.

Coping with Loss: Dreams of Prayagraj Shattered

The realization that I couldn't return to Prayagraj for at least nine months hit me like a heavy blow. The house I had lovingly decorated, the serene spiritual atmosphere that had become a part of me, the imagined sounds of temple bells and morning birdsong—all faded into distant memories. These were the elements of a life I had dreamed of, where I believed

I would thrive mentally and spiritually. Now, abruptly, these dreams were shattered.

The loss was profound. I had to set aside my plans for a new beginning in Prayagraj, where I had hoped to find solace and renewal. The environment I thought would shape my future positively was suddenly beyond reach. It was a heartbreaking realization, leaving me grappling with a sense of emptiness and uncertainty about what lay ahead.

As I came to terms with this reality, I found myself mourning not just the physical distance from Prayagraj, but also the emotional distance from the life I had envisioned there. The vibrant colors of anticipation had dulled into shades of resignation, as I navigated through each day with a longing for the place and the dreams that now seemed suspended in time

The CT Scan Experience: Witnessing Others' Pain

Before my scheduled CT scan, I made my way to the lab, where I encountered a scene that would stay with me forever. A young boy, accompanied by his mother, sat quietly in the waiting area. Curious, I inquired, only to learn the devastating truth—he had brain cancer. The weight of this news hit me hard as I witnessed his mother's inconsolable grief, her cries echoing through the sterile halls. Tears welled in my eyes, overwhelmed by the raw emotion and the stark reality of their plight.

This encounter left an indelible mark on me, amplifying my own fears about what lay ahead. As I waited for my turn in the scanning room, dread crept over me—not just of the procedure itself, but of the potential diagnosis that could evoke the same anguish in my own loved ones. The thought of my mother enduring such pain gnawed at my resolve.

When I finally lay inside the scanner, the metallic hum seemed to amplify my anxious thoughts. "What if it's cancer?" I wondered, grappling with existential questions that haunted me through the night. "Is death the worst that could happen?"

These thoughts circled in my mind, a silent storm of fear and introspection, as the machine scanned my body. Each moment in that sterile chamber brought me closer to confronting my deepest fears, and to grappling with the uncertain path ahead.

A Night of Reflection: Contemplating Life and Death

That night, in the silence of the house, I grappled with conflicting thoughts. I questioned how something like this could happen to someone who took extreme care of their health. This question plagued my mind, as I tried to understand why and how this had happened to me. During video calls with my beloved, even though she was far away in Delhi, I could sense her fast heartbeats and deep concern. I loved her and my family very much, and I had wanted to achieve great things for their happiness, respect, and pride.

But now, circumstances had thrown me down, and I feared I might soon merge with the ground after death.

As I lay there, I thought about how I didn't want to die slowly and painfully. I imagined going to Uttarakhand, sitting on the side of a big mountain, talking to myself, remembering all the beautiful events of my life, and thanking Lord Krishna for deciding to call me to his shelter so soon. I wanted my death, if it were to come, to be a beautiful one - not an end, but a new beginning.

That night, there came a point when I embraced every situation and became extremely carefree about any kind of future. However, the people connected to me were not ready to let me go so soon. They denied my desire to be free, wanting to see me alive and healthy, and were making every possible effort to ensure that.

Good News and Bad: Test Results and Ongoing Struggles

The following day, my sister went to the hospital to collect the results of my cancer and CT scans. She later described how her hands trembled with anticipation as she waited for the reports. To our immense relief, the findings brought a mix of good news and challenges. The reports confirmed that there was no cancer detected, a huge weight lifted off our shoulders.

Additionally, they indicated that my lung capacity was surprisingly robust. However, amidst this relief, there was also sobering news—the scans revealed a significant and troubling lung infection that demanded immediate attention.

Dr. Rajeev Kakkad wasted no time in devising a comprehensive treatment plan based on these results. In the initial days of treatment, there was a noticeable improvement, and I began to feel some relief. However, on the eleventh day, a setback occurred—I once again coughed up blood. This development shook our hopes, but Dr. Rajeev calmly reassured us that such occurrences were normal during the treatment process. He emphasized the importance of persistence and patience in managing the infection effectively.

Navigating these highs and lows became our new reality—grappling with the gratitude of avoiding a cancer diagnosis while confronting the ongoing challenges posed by the persistent lung infection. Each day brought a mix of hope and concern, as we relied on Dr. Rajeev's expertise and steadfast guidance to navigate the uncertain road ahead.

May 14th: A Day of Celebration Turns Critical

Despite grappling with ongoing health challenges, we were steadfast in our determination to celebrate my parents' marriage anniversary on May 13th. Both my beloved and I had eagerly contributed to the preparations, looking forward to cherishing this special occasion together. Plans were also in place for Mother's Day on May 14th, with my sister taking charge of most arrangements, ensuring everything was perfect.

However, fate had its own abrupt plans. On the morning of May 14th, during a video call with my beloved while resting in bed, an unsettling sensation gripped my chest—a foreboding sign that blood was about to erupt. What followed was an overwhelming surge, more profuse than any prior episode, shocking everyone present. My beloved, witnessing this harrowing event through the video call, was rendered speechless by the severity of the scene.

Realizing the gravity of the situation, I found myself uttering thoughts that shattered the momentary silence: this could mark the culmination of my journey, the unanticipated moment to bid a final farewell. The anguish etched on my mother's face and the heart-rending sound of her cries echoed through the room.

Tears streamed down my cheeks as freely as the blood flowed from my chest, a stark reminder of life's unpredictability and the fragility of human existence.

Rush to the Hospital: The Most Difficult Journey

In that critical moment, my sister displayed remarkable wisdom by deciding to rush me to the hospital without delay. Despite the hospital being 10 kilometers away from our home, every kilometer felt like an eternity. I lay in the car, trying desperately to minimize the flow of blood. Even the slightest jolt during the journey caused excruciating pain and discomfort.

After what seemed like an agonizing half-hour journey, we finally arrived at the hospital. Those were undoubtedly the most challenging moments of my life.

Upon our arrival, the medical team sprang into action, immediately assessing the gravity of my condition. They bombarded me with questions, probing for clues to the cause. One of their inquiries focused on my daily cigarette consumption which was zero, attempting to decipher any potential triggers for my current state. As I responded to their queries, my coughing fits resumed, and before long, the blood vomiting exceeded all previous instances.

Witnessing the severity of my condition, a female doctor commented gravely that under similar circumstances, many would not have survived losing so much blood. Her words underscored the direness of my situation. Swiftly, I was ushered onto a hospital bed, where urgent treatment commenced without delay.

Ten Days in the Hospital: A Battle for Recovery

That first night in the hospital was a whirlwind of urgency and treatment. I received six injections to stem the severe bleeding, each one a lifeline in my battle for survival. Physically drained and weaker than ever before, even the smallest movement threatened to trigger another wave of blood loss. My family stood vigilantly by my bedside, their presence a constant source of comfort amidst the turmoil.

To manage the relentless bleeding, tissue paper napkins became a daily necessity. They spared me the repeated trips to the dustbin, allowing me to handle the immediate aftermath of blood episodes right where I lay. The bleeding was so intense that we would exhaust an entire packet of napkins in just one day. I remember one instance vividly—during a coughing fit, blood inadvertently splattered onto my sister. Her response was a testament to her unwavering support and care, brushing it off as she continued to tend to me.

Throughout my stay, medical interventions were frequent and essential. Due to complications from infection, the placement of VIGO (IV lines) in my hands became a painful ordeal. Allergic reactions necessitated their removal and replacement at least fifteen times, leaving my hands swollen, red, and throbbing with pain.

Despite these daunting challenges, the meticulous care of Dr. Avdhesh and the medical team began to yield positive signs of progress. Each day marked a small victory in my recovery journey, reassuring us that we were moving in the right direction amidst the uncertainty and discomfort of hospital life.

Returning Home: The Long Road to Health

After enduring a challenging ten-day hospital stay, the medical team finally deemed me well enough for discharge. It marked the end of a critical phase but also signaled the start of a long and uncertain road to recovery. Those ten days were transformative, reshaping my outlook on life in profound ways. Amid the clinical environment of the hospital, I came to a stark realization: all the aspirations and pursuits in life hinge fundamentally on one essential pillar—good health.

Throughout my hospitalization, I grappled with physical weakness that made even the simplest tasks daunting. For those ten days, I relied on a wheelchair to navigate the sterile corridors and bustling wards, a constant reminder of my diminished strength. Each push of the wheels underscored the fragility of my condition and the steep uphill journey ahead to reclaim vitality.

The experience etched deep lessons into my consciousness. It taught me that true enjoyment of life's offerings—whether pursuing passions or cherishing moments with loved ones—is only possible when one's body and mind are in harmony. It reshaped my priorities, focusing my energies not on material pursuits or external achievements, but on the singular goal of regaining my health.

Leaving the hospital, I carried with me a newfound appreciation for the resilience of the human body and the importance of prioritizing well-being above all else. It was a journey that extended far beyond physical recuperation, encompassing a renewed commitment to nurturing both body and spirit, ensuring they thrive together.

Six Months of Treatment: Family Support and Healing

Upon returning home from the hospital, the next phase of my recovery spanned six months of intensive treatment. Supported by the unwavering dedication of my family, each day became a testament to their profound care and steadfast support. They anticipated my needs with intuitive grace, ensuring I had everything necessary for my physical comfort and emotional well-being.

The treatment regimen was demanding, requiring strict adherence to medications, frequent medical consultations, and diligent monitoring of symptoms.

Despite the physical challenges, their presence provided a sense of security and reassurance that bolstered my spirits during the toughest moments. Their unwavering optimism and encouragement became a guiding light through the ups and downs of recovery.

Beyond the tangible support, their emotional support played a pivotal role in my healing journey. Their presence was a constant reminder of hope and resilience, turning what could have been a period of despair into one of determination and perseverance. Their unwavering faith in my recovery mirrored my own resolve to overcome the challenges posed by my health condition.

Over the course of those six months, I witnessed incremental progress in my health. Each milestone achieved—whether it was a reduction in symptoms, improved energy levels, or moments of reprieve from discomfort—was a testament to their unwavering commitment and the effectiveness of the treatment plan.

In the end, their dedication and the comprehensive care I received at home proved to be the cornerstone of my recovery. Their love and support not only nurtured my physical healing but also fortified my spirit, laying the foundation for a renewed sense of well-being and optimism for the future.

Two Years Later: Reflections on Life, Death, and Belonging

It's been two years since that life-altering experience, and I am grateful to stand here today, fully healed and healthy. The journey I underwent was marked by intense pain, but it also became a profound teacher, imparting lessons that have forever changed me.

The ordeal forced me to confront my deepest fears and attachments, particularly my fear of death and my clinging to life's transient pleasures. In the crucible of uncertainty and suffering, I learned to release these fears and attachments, realizing that true peace comes from accepting the natural cycles of existence.

My perspective on life and death underwent a seismic shift. I now perceive death not as an endpoint, but as a transition—an evolution from one form of existence to another. This understanding has brought me a profound sense of tranquillity and acceptance, enabling me to embrace the mysteries beyond our physical world with a newfound clarity.

I've come to cherish each moment as a gift, recognizing the impermanence of life and the preciousness of every breath. This awareness has deepened my connection to the universe and illuminated the interconnectedness of all living beings.

In closing, I reflect on a quote that encapsulates my evolved worldview:

"Death may end me in this world, but not in the realm from where I truly belong."

This experience, though agonizing, has gifted me with a profound sense of purpose and belonging in the grand tapestry of existence.

It 'S Remain Uncertain
(Bornali Ray)

The Unvarnished Canvas of Destiny: A Daughter's Tale

This is not a tale spun from the threads of a novel, nor a scene stolen from the silver screen; this is the raw, unfiltered narrative of my life, a canvas painted with the hues of reality and the brushstrokes of fate. My story begins thus: I am the proud daughter of my parents, a jewel in the crown of their legacy. By profession, I am a teacher, a sculptor of minds, and also a perpetual student, forever a seeker of knowledge. Currently, I am pursuing a Bachelor of Education at Jamia Millia Islamia in Delhi, a city renowned for its aspirations and dreams, where I have journeyed to sit for my exams.

The day of my departure was a kaleidoscope of emotions. I embraced my family and friends with heartfelt goodbyes, their faces a gallery of mixed emotions—pride in my pursuit, concern for my journey, and unwavering support. However, amidst the flurry of farewells, one absence weighed heavily on my heart: my father. A police officer, he embodies courage and dedication, often consumed

by the demands of his duty—a hero in uniform
whose strength and sacrifice form the backbone
of our family's foundation.

I longed to see him before leaving, to feel the
reassuring warmth of his presence and to share a
moment that would linger in my memory. Yet, as
fate would have it, he was

ensnared in the labyrinth of his responsibilities,
and our farewell transpired through the faint echo
of his voice over the phone. In that fleeting
exchange, amidst the backdrop of departure, our
unspoken bond spoke volumes—the admiration, the
unyielding support, and the shared understanding
of the paths we tread.

As I embarked on my journey to Delhi, each step
forward resonated with a deeper meaning. It
wasn't just about academic pursuits; it was a
metamorphosis of our relationship—a daughter's
pursuit of knowledge mirroring her father's
commitment to duty. Despite the physical distance,
our connection grew stronger, illuminated by the
profound threads that weave through the canvas
of destiny.

In the crucible of separation, our narrative evolved, etched with the resilience and shared determination that define our journey together. Each moment away from home became a testament to the unwavering bond between a daughter and her father, painted on the unvarnished canvas of life's intricate tapestry.

The Invisible Lifeline: A Father's Distant Vigil

Upon my arrival in Delhi, my father's call cut through the cacophony of the city to ask if I had reached safely. He has this peculiar habit: when I'm at home, he barely checks on me, like a shadow that never questions the light. But when I

am away, he calls incessantly, like a lighthouse beacon, asking if I've eaten, if I'm alright. Sometimes, he calls at 4 AM, and I, frustrated and bleary-eyed, would say, "Dad, please, let me sleep," and end the call, his concern an anchor in the tempest of my life.

It was the fourth day of my sojourn in Delhi. The city had already begun to weave itself into my daily life, each day adding a new layer to my experience. After completing my university work, I ventured out to eat and gather materials for my project, the city's pulse synchronizing with mine. It was November in Delhi, a time when the city wears its charm with an effortless grace. The streets were alive with the symphony of life, the air thick with the aroma of street food and the hum of countless conversations.

People gathered at tea stalls, each a character in the sprawling novel that is Delhi. The sky, heavy with the promise of rain, whispered secrets in a gentle drizzle, and as evening approached, the heavens transformed into a canvas of twilight hues. The orange and pink hues of the sunset bled into the horizon, creating a serene backdrop to the city's vibrant energy. Flocks of birds crossed the sky, stitching the horizon with their graceful flight as they made their way home.

I felt myself falling for this city, entangled in its embrace like a lover in a passionate dance.

Each moment in Delhi was rich with discovery and connection, the city's rhythm blending seamlessly with my own.

And through it all, my father's distant vigilance remained a constant, his calls a silent lifeline that anchored me amidst the swirl of new experiences.

The Call That Shattered the Illusion of Forever

Just then, my phone rang, shattering my reverie like a stone through glass. "Hello, sister, Dad is not feeling well. We're taking him to the doctor," my sister's voice, urgent and clipped, was a dagger through my heart. I stood still, the world a dizzying blur around me. Just yesterday, everything seemed fine. My father had said, "I don't feel good when you're not at home. Come back soon." His words now echoed with a haunting prescience. What changed so suddenly? A second call pierced through my confusion: "Sister, Dad had a brain stroke. Come as soon as possible." In the chilling November air, my body blazed like a wildfire, my heart thundered like a storm, sweat trickled like molten fear down my forehead, and tears carved desperate paths down my cheeks. A scream lay trapped within my chest, strangled by disbelief. Life is a cruel artist, unpredictable in its strokes, a relentless painter of sorrow and joy. I couldn't accept the reality; it felt like a tragic scene from a movie, or a nightmare from which I would awaken and find everything restored.

But this wasn't fiction or a fleeting dream. This was the harsh, unyielding truth, the living narrative of my life, a story written in the ink of anguish and the paper of time.

Marionette of Fate: Dancing to Life's Cruel Tune

I was a marionette in the hands of fate, my strings taut with tension, my heart a fragile vessel sailing through the storm of uncertainty. The city's bustling streets now seemed like a cruel mockery of my anguish. Each step I took was a heavy burden, every breath a desperate grasp for normalcy in a world turned upside down. A month and four days have gone by since I arrived in Guwahati, and during this time, life has taught me many lessons. In the book of life, there are pages for which I was never prepared, full of stories more complex than I ever imagined.

Just a month ago, my life was peaceful, untouched by sadness, as I lived under the protective shade of my father. His presence was a shield, sheltering me from the storms of the world, allowing me to float through life with a sense of security and ease. But no one can escape the passing of time. Time changed, and like dark clouds covering a clear sky, a heavy storm swept into my life. The tranquility I once took for granted was shattered, replaced by a whirlwind of confusion and grief.

At first, I was overwhelmed by this storm. I cried
and felt lost, unable to accept the harsh reality
that had been thrust upon me.

It was as if the strings of my marionette self had
been cut, leaving me to collapse into a heap, unable
to move, unable to think. The pain was unbearable,
a constant reminder of the fragile nature of
happiness and the ever-present shadow of sorrow.

Slowly, however, I adapted to my new life, like
water taking the shape of its container. I began to
navigate the turbulent waters of my existence with
a newfound resilience, my heart still fragile but
now encased in a shell of determination. I started
to see the world through different eyes, each day
revealing new facets of struggle and perseverance
that I had never before appreciated.

I used to think my daily problems were big, each
challenge a mountain too high to climb. But now, I
realize what true struggles are. My earlier worries
seemed trivial, mere pebbles on the path of life
compared to the boulders that now obstructed my
way. The harsh reality of life in Guwahati, with its
constant reminders of impermanence and change,
taught me to embrace the unpredictable dance of
fate, to sway with the rhythm of life's cruel tune.

In this city, each day has been a lesson in survival, a test of endurance that has reshaped my understanding of strength and resilience. The streets, once filled with an overwhelming chaos, have become a reflection of my own internal battles, each step forward a victory over the shadows that threaten to consume me.

And though my strings may still be pulled by the whims of fate, I now dance with a grace and strength born of hardship and acceptance, my heart a testament to the power of enduring through the storms of life.

The Hospital: A Labyrinth of Human Agony

One day, I went to a pharmacy near GMCH to get medicine for my father. As I waited, I witnessed a scene that pierced through the numbing routine of hospital visits—a woman who had sold her jewelry was pleading for medicine for her husband. Her desperation was palpable, a stark reflection of the human suffering that pervaded the hospital. The bed next to my father's seemed cursed; every patient I saw there had died. I heard their painful cries and saw their families praying desperately to God—some to Allah, others to Krishna. These prayers were not for wealth or material things but for the lives of their loved ones. It made me wonder if God could really be so uncaring, turning a deaf ear to such profound agony.

I saw the struggles in the ICU and dialysis wards, where the air was thick with despair. The doctors, who seemed like gods, performed their check-ups with a clinical detachment, their faces a mask of calm amidst the storm of human suffering. In the eyes of ordinary people,

I saw a kaleidoscope of emotions: fear, sadness, hope, and longing. Each face told a story of sleepless nights, of battles fought against unseen foes, as they anxiously awaited the results that could change their lives forever.

On the floors of GMCH, the truth of human vulnerability was laid bare. I had heard that people are controlled by circumstances, but here, I saw this truth etched in the lines of worry on every face. Like the endless stream of devotees at a temple, I saw a continuous flow of people in every office at GMCH, desperately trying to submit their reports. Their eyes reflected a deep yearning for sleep, their lips cracked from thirst, their bodies tormented by hunger. The relentless march to submit paperwork was a testament to their endurance and a stark contrast to my own understanding of life's hardships.

I thought I knew what struggle was from my own experiences, but the scenes at GMCH opened my eyes to a level of human suffering I had never imagined. The endless rush for reports, the desperate prayers, and the silent pleas of those waiting for a miracle were all reminders of the fragile line that separates life from death. It was a stark lesson in humility, a painful reminder that in the grand labyrinth of human agony, we are all mere marionettes, dancing to the cruel tune of fate.

The Price of Life: Selling Dreams to Buy Time

The financial strain of my father's medical care became overwhelming. We found ourselves in a desperate situation, forced to make heart-wrenching decisions. With tears in our eyes, we sold my father's beloved motorcycle—the very one he had proudly ridden to work each day. The sight of it being taken away felt like watching a piece of him leave us, a painful separation that echoed through our hearts.

But it wasn't enough. We had to go further, selling parcels of our ancestral land. Each sale felt like we were trading away pieces of our family's history and future, each transaction a heavy blow to our sense of identity and security. The land, once a symbol of stability and legacy, became a commodity to be sacrificed in exchange for fleeting moments of hope.

I found myself in the hospital corridors, not just as a worried daughter, but as a desperate supplicant. I pleaded with doctors, nurses, and anyone who would listen for help, for discounts, for any relief from the mounting medical bills that threatened to drown us. The shame of our circumstances burned deep within, a constant reminder of our vulnerability and the precariousness of life itself.

These sacrifices and humiliations were a cruel testament to how quickly life can change, how swiftly security can crumble into desperation. Each day became a battle fought not just against illness, but against the relentless tide of financial ruin. Yet amidst the anguish and loss, there was a fierce determination—a resolve to do whatever it took to buy more time, to cling to the hope that each sacrifice would pave the way for another day with my father.

In the end, the price of life was measured not just in monetary terms, but in the dreams we sold, the lands we surrendered, and the dignity we sacrificed. It was a painful reckoning with the reality that love and resilience alone cannot always shield us from the merciless demands of fate. And as we navigated this harrowing journey, I learned that the true cost of survival is often paid in the currency of our deepest bonds and most cherished memories.

The Hospital: A Stage for Life's Greatest Drama

As days passed, the hospital unfolded like a never-ending drama, each scene revealing the raw emotions of those within its walls. Every day brought a whirlwind of emotions—people running, crying, and praying, their faces etched with struggles and hopes that mirrored my own. Mothers cradled sick babies, their eyes filled with a mixture of fear and determination. Elderly patients gripped the rails of their beds with trembling hands, their frailty a stark contrast to their resilience.

Fathers paced corridors with worried expressions, their thoughts consumed by the well-being of their loved ones.

The hospital felt like a battlefield, each person fighting their own war against illness and uncertainty. It was a place where strength and vulnerability intertwined, where the human spirit shone brightest amidst adversity. Amidst the pain and turmoil, I witnessed acts of courage and compassion that reaffirmed my belief in the resilience of the human heart.

The hospital's harsh, cold light cast everything in a pale, sickly hue, amplifying the stark reality of life and death that played out daily. The air was heavy with the clinical scent of medicine and disinfectant, a constant reminder of the sterile environment that surrounded us. Nurses and doctors moved with purposeful urgency, their faces marked by fatigue but their dedication unwavering. The rhythmic sounds of beeping machines, the cries of infants, and the whispered prayers of families formed a symphony of hope and despair that filled the air.

In this environment where every second mattered, fear mingled with hope in equal measure. It was a place where life hung in delicate balance, where each heartbeat and each breath held profound significance. The hospital became a microcosm of the human experience—a testament to our capacity to endure, to love, and to hope against all odds. And amidst the chaos and uncertainty, I found solace in the shared humanity that bound us all together, united in our collective struggle for healing and survival.

Midnight in the Garden of Life and Death

It was a bitter December night, the hospital cloaked in an icy silence that mirrored the winter outside. At 2 AM, I found myself immersed in the solemn rhythm of the hospital, tending to everything related to my father's care. The air was cold and serious, every corridor a passage fraught with the weight of life and death.

In that stillness, I witnessed a scene that shook me to the core—a young man, about 23 years old, violently vomiting in the bed next to my father's. The stark contrast of his youth and the intensity of his suffering pierced through the sterile atmosphere. Inquiry revealed a chilling truth: he had attempted to end his life by drinking phenyl, a desperate act that reverberated with a profound sense of despair.

Anger surged within me like a tempest. He was young, married, with a baby boy—a life entwined with responsibilities and love, yet he had chosen to abandon it all. His wife stood beside him, her face a canvas of raw emotion—tears mingled with anger, disbelief mixed with disappointment. Her voice, harsh and broken, carried the weight of shattered dreams and unfulfilled promises.

It felt like an unfair duel between life and death unfolding before my eyes. On one side, the relentless fight to preserve a cherished life, on the other, a tragic surrender to hopelessness.

The hospital corridors echoed with the clash of these stark realities, each moment a poignant reminder of the fragility and preciousness of life.

In that chilling hour, amidst the battle for survival and the anguish of loss, I grasped the profound truth that life is a delicate thread, easily frayed yet resilient in its essence. The scene etched itself into my memory—a haunting reflection of the depths of human despair and the enduring struggle for hope against all odds.

The Great Paradox: Fighting for Life, Fleeing from It

I couldn't fathom why someone would choose to extinguish their own existence when life itself is so invaluable. Witnessing my father's courageous struggle against illness underscored for me the immense worth of life and the relentless strength required to fight for it. It was a profound juxtaposition—the determination of one man to survive amidst the backdrop of another's despair.

In that moment, the hospital walls seemed to close in around me, bearing witness to these contrasting battles. On one side, the unwavering fight for life—a testament to human resilience and the will to endure. On the other, a tragic attempt to flee from life's burdens—a stark reminder of the depths of human desperation.

My father's own battle hung in the balance between life and death. It was a surreal experience, seeing him in the ICU, his face adorned with an oxygen mask, his hand connected to an IV drip—a scene that until then, I had only encountered in films. The sight was heart-wrenching, a stark reminder of the fragility of life and the harsh realities of mortality.

For the first time in my life, I found myself offering a heartfelt prayer to God—a plea borne of desperation and hope: "Please save my father's life, Lord!"

And miraculously, God heard my prayer.

The Long Road Back: A Father's Slow Recovery

As weeks turned into months, my father's physical condition began a gradual ascent toward improvement. Though his speech remains altered, now spoken slowly and with deep contemplation, his gaze holds a profound longing as he navigates his daily existence. There are moments of distress—a sudden scream, an attempt to remove the saline pipe, hands stained with blood from unintended actions, and occasional bouts of vomiting during meals. Each day unfolds as a testament to the fragility of life and the unwavering resilience demanded of us in the face of adversity.

I find myself darting from one doctor to the next, seeking answers in a quest tinged with both hope and despair.

My prayers to God echo with a poignant plea: "How much more suffering, Lord?"

And so, four arduous months pass. My father's condition stabilizes, yet the specter of his former self remains uncertain. These months have tested me in ways I could never have imagined. Despite my role as a teacher, I have come to understand that life itself is the ultimate educator, imparting lessons with every twist and turn. As the eldest daughter, the weight of household responsibilities falls squarely upon my shoulders. My mother, always hoping for my maturity, now sees it forged in the crucible of adversity.

I have grown up.

Though pain lingers, tears have hardened into resolve. I have become the pillar of strength for my family, shouldering my father's duties with a silent determination. In the quietude of our home, I have become a shadow, a steadfast presence in the midst of uncertainty and recovery.

These months have reshaped me, teaching me the profound truth that strength emerges not from unyielding toughness, but from the quiet acceptance and resilience nurtured by love and responsibility. And as I continue down this long road back, I carry with me the lessons learned from the crucible of suffering, each step a testament to the enduring power of the human spirit.

Dreams Deferred, Life Cherished

Looking back, I recall my father's cherished dreams: to retire peacefully at home, to tend a garden blooming with his favorite flowers, to wander distant lands, and to savor the warmth of festivals surrounded by loved ones. These aspirations, now mere echoes of what could have been, remain unfulfilled. Yet, I carry no regrets, for his mere existence, his every breath, is a priceless gift that fills our hearts with gratitude. He remains our unwavering father, a pillar of strength and love.

But amidst this gratitude lies a poignant ache—the absence of his 4 AM calls, once a steadfast connection through the quiet hours. Time slips away unnoticed as we postpone plans, delay wearing new clothes for a special occasion, and push off meaningful moments for a more convenient tomorrow. It's a haunting reminder of how swiftly life passes us by.

So, my dear friends, cherish the present. Embrace each fleeting moment of joy and connection, for life's tapestry is woven with threads of unpredictable beauty and sorrow. Mend relationships with those estranged, for reconciliation cannot wait for an uncertain future. And above all, prioritize the precious time you share with family, for it is in these bonds that true wealth and meaning reside.

For who can predict when, where, or how swiftly the curtain will fall on our dreams and aspirations?

In these reflections, I find a bittersweet clarity—a call to seize every precious second, to embrace life's complexities, and to honor the legacy of love and resilience that defines our journey.

A Bottle Of Acid
(Haidar Hashmi)

A BOTTLE OF ACID

Love at First Sight: A Wedding That Changed Everything

November 14, 2019, was a day that would change my life forever. It was my sister's wedding, a joyous occasion filled with laughter and celebration. Amidst the whirlwind of festivities, I saw her. Time seemed to stand still as our eyes met across the crowded room. She left an indelible impression on my soul, her presence electric and captivating. Silently, my heart rejoiced, lost in thoughts of her. Her very existence made this wedding unforgettable, her image forever etched in my mind. But fate, in its cruel wisdom, kept us apart that night. We didn't speak, didn't meet. I was left wondering if she had even noticed me, a quiet observer in the sea of guests.

From Instagram to Real Life: A Modern Love Story Unfolds

Time passed with agonizing slowness, each day a reminder of what could have been. Then, like a bolt from the blue, destiny intervened. A message appeared on my Instagram, and my heart skipped a beat. It was her - the girl from the wedding. Joy and disbelief warred within me as I read her words. I was both elated and stunned into silence. This serendipitous connection felt like a miracle, a stroke of luck so profound it left me breathless.

Her reaching out to me was nothing short of a blessing from the universe. Our online conversations blossomed into a digital romance. With each message, we drew closer, our connection deepening. The virtual world became our sanctuary, a place where we could bare our souls without fear. As we got to know each other, our feelings grew stronger, more intense. The screen between us couldn't dampen the electricity of our budding relationship. Finally, we made the momentous decision to meet in person, to bridge the gap between the digital and the real.

The Orphanage Meeting: Discovering Her Past and Our Future

Breaking from convention, we chose a place steeped in her history - the Sakina Girls Home Orphanage. This wasn't just any location; it was where she had completed her education up to tenth grade. The choice spoke volumes about her past - a father lost in childhood, an uneducated mother unable to guide her future. This place had been her sanctuary, her crucible. It had shaped her, molded her into the woman who now captivated me. By choosing this place, she was inviting me into her world, sharing a piece of her soul.

Our first meeting was electric, charged with the energy of shared understanding and mutual respect. The connection we had forged online translated beautifully into the real world. We grew very close to each other, seeing each other with new eyes, full of admiration and affection.

Our love blossomed rapidly, nurtured by our genuine connection. In that moment, we made a silent vow to always stay together, our hearts intertwined by an invisible thread of destiny.

January 11, 2020, marked the beginning of our series of meetings. Each encounter brought us closer, as we talked for hours, learning about each other's hopes, dreams, and fears. We tried to understand each other completely, peeling back layers of our personalities to reveal our true selves.

Moonlit Magic: A Perfect Night on Alibag Beach

One moonlit night on Alibag beach stands out in my memory like a perfect photograph. The silvery light danced on the waves, mirroring the sparkle in our eyes. As we sat side by side on the cool sand, the rhythmic lapping of the waves seemed to echo the beating of our hearts. The moon's reflection shimmered in the sea, touching our feet with each wave, illuminating them with an otherworldly glow. The sparkle in the waves found its way into our hearts, filling us with a joy so pure it was almost tangible. That night, we melted into each other like the moonlight melting into the sea, two souls becoming one under the vast, star-studded sky.

The Shoe Gift: Realizing Material Things Can't Match Her Love

In a moment of spontaneity at the Sea Woods Grand Central mall in Navi Mumbai, I stumbled upon what I thought was the perfect gift - a pair of shoes that seemed made for her. The moment I saw them, I knew they belonged on her feet. Without hesitation, I had them wrapped and sent to her. But as I reflected on this gesture, I realized the inadequacy of material gifts.

How could any object, no matter how beautiful,
compare to the priceless gift she had given me?
She had reshaped my entire world, turning even
the most mundane things into objects of beauty.
Her love was my armor against life's hardships, her
presence my strength in times of weakness. She
was like my shoulders, giving me the power to face
any challenge that came my way.

The perspective she gave me transformed
everything that once seemed hurtful or bad into
something beautiful and meaningful.

When Love Turns Sour: Fighting and Silence Take Over

But life, ever the cruel playwright, had other plans
for our love story. Like a snake in the garden,
misunderstandings began to creep in, poisoning our
once-pure connection. What started as small
disagreements snowballed into full-blown fights.
The love that had once flowed so freely between
us began to ebb, replaced by anger and
resentment. Eventually, the unthinkable happened -
we stopped talking altogether.

Lockdown Loneliness: COVID-19 Adds to the Pain

As if our personal troubles weren't enough, the world was plunged into chaos by the COVID-19 pandemic. Forced to stay in our homes, the physical distance between us seemed to mirror the emotional chasm that had opened up. The isolation gnawed at my soul, each day without her a fresh torment. I was alone, yet surrounded by the suffocating presence of my own thoughts and regrets.

During this time, I was constantly suffocating, dying inside. As the distance between us kept increasing, I was moving away from myself, losing touch with the person I had become with her. The world around me, once full of color and life, now seemed gray and lifeless.

A Desperate Act: Drinking Acid to End the Pain

Then, in a moment of utter despair, I made a decision that would alter the course of my life forever. Feeling that I would now be free from this suffocating existence, I decided to end my life. With a heart heavy with sorrow and a mind clouded by desperation, I locked myself in the bathroom and drank more than half a bottle of hydrochloric acid. The pain that followed was beyond anything I had ever experienced or could have imagined. As soon as the acid touched my lips, it felt like I had swallowed liquid fire.

I collapsed to the ground with a thunderous thud, my body convulsing in agony. It felt as if someone had thrust a burning mountain inside me, like the lava of a volcano was coursing through my veins instead of blood. Every part of my body seemed to be slowly melting, dissolving, burning from the inside out. The pain was so intense, so all-encompassing, that I writhed on the floor like a fish out of water, gasping for breath that wouldn't come.

Family to the Rescue: A Frantic Rush to the Hospital

The sound of my fall alerted my family. They rushed to the bathroom door, pounding on it with increasing desperation as they realized something was terribly wrong. My mother, my two younger sisters, my father - all of them were there, their voices a cacophony of fear and concern. My father, being a technician, had tools at his disposal. He used them to force the door open, revealing the horrifying scene within.

As soon as the door swung open, everyone was struck dumb with shock at my condition. My mother and sisters, in a desperate attempt to help, began pouring water down my throat, hoping against hope that it might dilute the acid or provide some relief. But it was futile. Blood poured from my mouth in a constant stream, likely from internal organs that had been ravaged by the corrosive liquid.

Despite the excruciating pain and the chaos around me, I was eerily aware of everything happening. I could hear every word, feel every touch, even as my body rebelled against me. In a moment of anger and despair that I'll never forget, my father uttered words that cut deeper than any physical pain: "You had a desire to die, now it's better if you just die."

In the midst of this crisis, my family seemed to lose all sense of direction. They didn't know what to do, how to help. In their desperation, they even sought help from neighbors. Finally, they managed to get me into an auto-rickshaw and rushed me to the hospital.

The journey to find medical help was a nightmare within a nightmare. We first arrived at DY Patil Hospital, but they refused to admit me, saying they were only taking COVID patients. Panic rising, my family then had to transport me to Sion Medical Centre, a grueling 25-kilometer journey made even more difficult by the pandemic lockdown. Transportation was a huge challenge, but somehow, we managed to find another auto-rickshaw to take us there.

The Hospital Horror: Fighting for Life Amid the Pandemic

At Sion Medical Centre, I was immediately admitted to the emergency ward. They gave me a liquid to drink - some kind of medicine that induced violent vomiting.

The purpose was to expel as much of the acid as possible from my system. After this, they began an ECG to monitor my heart, which must have been under tremendous stress. More of the vomit-inducing liquid was administered, causing me to retch repeatedly. Finally, they gave me an injection that plunged me into unconsciousness.

Even in my unconscious state, some part of my mind remained eerily alert. I could sense my mother and sister crying beside me, their sobs a testament to their anguish. I was aware of relatives coming to visit, discussing my condition in hushed, worried tones. I could feel my father's presence too, sitting silently to one side, perhaps still processing the shock of what had happened. But while my mind was semi-conscious, my body was anything but still. My family later told me that I twitched and convulsed, and that pained groans escaped my lips, a physical manifestation of the agony I was enduring.

During these two harrowing days, my father was kept in police custody. He was subjected to intense interrogation, asked over and over what could have driven his son to attempt suicide. The police, looking for answers, even resorted to mental torture. Although my father didn't know the exact reason for my drastic action, he made an educated guess. He told the police that perhaps my relationship with my beloved had ended, leading me to this desperate act.

After two days of hovering between life and death, I finally opened my eyes fully and regained consciousness. But the scene that greeted me was like something out of a nightmare.

All around me were corpses wrapped in black polythene, lined up in rows. These were the victims of the raging COVID-19 pandemic, a stark reminder of the fragility of life and the cruel timing of my own brush with death.

Slow Recovery: Feeding Tubes and Shocking Changes

As I came out of my unconscious state, I was moved to the ICU ward. The doctors continued to monitor me closely, regularly testing me for COVID-19 as well. The acid had scorched my insides so badly that I couldn't eat or drink anything. Even the slightest attempt to put something in my mouth caused excruciating pain due to the extensive internal wounds. To keep me nourished, they inserted a tube through my nose that connected directly to my stomach. This tube became my lifeline, delivering liquid nutrition directly to my stomach, bypassing my ravaged throat and esophagus. This tube remained with me for about 30 days, a constant reminder of how close I had come to death.

I remained in the hospital for about 9 days, undergoing intensive treatment. When I was finally allowed to go home, the feeding tube came with me, a necessary evil for my continued recovery.

During this time, my physical appearance had changed so drastically that I was barely recognizable. I had withered away to skin and bones, a skeletal version of my former self. When relatives and friends would video call or see me, they would initially refuse to believe it was me. And when the reality sank in, they would break down in tears, shocked by my drastically altered appearance.

Silent Heartbreak: The One Who Never Came

But the deepest wound wasn't physical - it was emotional. Throughout this entire ordeal, the girl I had loved so deeply, the one for whom I had been willing to end my life, never reached out. She didn't come to see me in the hospital, didn't call to ask how I was doing. Her silence was deafening, more painful than any physical agony I had endured. The very person who had been the catalyst for all of this, for whom I had put myself in this condition, was breaking me even more with her indifference.

My mother, in an attempt to console me and help me move on, said, "You see, the one for whom you made such a condition of yourself didn't even come to see you, so now wake up and focus on yourself, focus on your future, focus on your health."

Battling Addiction: Turning to Harmful Habits

Time passed, and slowly, almost imperceptibly at first, my health started to improve. But as my body healed, my mind remained wounded. My life was trying to return to normal, but the memories of her haunted me. Depression set in, a heavy cloud that I couldn't shake off. In an attempt to numb the pain, I turned to addiction, developing habits that threatened to undo all the physical healing I had undergone.

Naya Savera: Seven Months of Tough Love and Growth

Seeing this destructive pattern, my family made a difficult decision. They sent me to a de-addiction center located in Vasai-Vihar, Maharashtra, named "Naya Savera Rehabilitation Centre". This would be my home for the next seven months, a place that would challenge me in ways I never thought possible.

The experience at Naya Savera was unlike anything an ordinary person could imagine. It was as if I had stepped into a different world, one with its own rules and reality. I often thought that I might have been better off in jail than in this place, a testament to how grueling the program was.

The therapies, while psychologically beneficial, felt like mental torture to someone unused to such intensive treatment.

I vividly remember being asked to sit facing the same wall for an entire day, my thoughts my only company. Other times, I would be made to mop the same spot on the floor for six hours straight, a lesson in patience and mindfulness that felt more like punishment. There were days when food was withheld entirely, with only water provided, pushing my body and mind to their limits.

One particularly challenging experience stands out in my memory. I was ordered to sleep on a floor where rainwater was constantly dripping heavily. It was uncomfortable, cold, and seemed pointless at the time. But as the days and weeks passed, I began to adapt to this harsh environment. I found reserves of strength I never knew I had, and I became ready to face whatever challenge each new day might bring.

Coming Home: Struggling to Fit Back into Normal Life

After seven long, grueling months, I was finally allowed to return home from the Rehabilitation Centre. But the transition was far from easy. Just as the world of the center had seemed alien when I first arrived, now the "real" world felt strange and overwhelming. I couldn't easily adapt to normal life because the effects of those months in rehabilitation were still deeply ingrained in me. The outside world, with its noise, its pace, and its complexities, felt overwhelming.

For about three months after my return, I stayed at home, completely quiet and isolated. I was trying to reconcile the person I had been before all of this with the person I had become. It was a period of deep introspection and adjustment.

A New Start: Friends and a Job at Bluestar

Then, like a lifeline thrown to a drowning man, some of my old friends reached out to me. They had been worried, wondering where I had disappeared to for so long. Their concern was touching, a reminder that I hadn't been forgotten by everyone. As soon as we met, they told me about a job opportunity - a technician position at a company called "Bluestar".

This opportunity felt like a gift from the universe. Since childhood, I had helped my father with his technical work, gaining a deep understanding of the field from a very young age. By the time I was 17 or 18, I had mastered many aspects of the work. Because of this background, I was able to secure the technician job immediately.

I worked at Bluestar for about 8 to 9 months. Getting this job was more than just employment - it was a symbol of hope, a sign that my life could get back on track. Before this, everything I had experienced had been incredibly painful.

The phase I had gone through was so severe that if someone else had endured it, they might not have survived.

Chasing Dreams: Landing a Job in the UAE

While working at Bluestar, a new ambition began to take root in my mind. I had always dreamed of working in the UAE, and I decided it was time to pursue that dream. With renewed determination, I sent my resume to more than 100 companies in the UAE. My persistence paid off when I received an email from a company asking if I was ready for an interview.

The day I had been waiting for had finally arrived. I prepared for the interview with all the energy and focus I could muster. Fortune smiled upon me - I passed the interview, and my job in my dream country was confirmed.

The company took care of all the formalities, confirmed my visa, and in September 2023, I found myself boarding a plane to the UAE. My heart was pounding with excitement and nervousness as I stepped onto the aircraft, ready to embark on this new chapter of my life.

The company that hired me is an educational firm called Reach, located in Abu Dhabi. They provide British education, and I joined them as a technician. Even today, I continue to work with them, filled with a sense of happiness and satisfaction that I never thought I'd feel again.

Finding Happiness: Gratitude and Family Pride

As I reflect on my journey - the dizzying highs, the crushing lows, the near-death experience, and the painful recovery - I'm filled with a profound sense of gratitude. Every experience, no matter how painful, has taught me valuable lessons. The challenges I've faced have forged me into a stronger, more resilient person. I've learned the importance of self-love, the value of true friendship, and the power of perseverance.

Today, I can say with certainty that I am extremely happy in my life. The biggest reason for this happiness is that my family is happy with me too. Seeing the pride and joy in their eyes makes all the struggles worthwhile. I will always remember what I've learned through these experiences, carrying these lessons with me as I continue to grow and thrive in my new life.

Looking back, I realize that my journey has been one of incredible transformation. From the heights of newfound love to the depths of despair, from the brink of death to a new life in a foreign land, I've traversed a path that few could imagine. Each step, each stumble, each triumph has contributed to shaping the person I am today.

The girl from the wedding, who once seemed like my whole world, is now a bittersweet memory. Her absence during my darkest hours taught me a painful but necessary lesson about the nature of true love and support. While the pain of her indifference once threatened to destroy me, it ultimately became a catalyst for my growth and self-discovery.

My family, who stood by me through the worst of times, has become an even more integral part of my life. Their unwavering support, even in the face of my most destructive behaviors, showed me the true meaning of unconditional love. The pride I see in their eyes now is a constant reminder of how far I've come and motivates me to continue striving for better.

My time at Naya Savera, though grueling, equipped me with the mental fortitude to face life's challenges head-on. The skills I learned there - patience, resilience, self-reflection - continue to serve me well in my personal and professional life.

Landing the job in the UAE feels like the culmination of all my struggles and efforts. It's not just a job; it's a symbol of my rebirth, a testament to my ability to rise from the ashes of my past and build a new, fulfilling life.

As I go about my days in Abu Dhabi, working at Reach and exploring this new chapter of my life, I'm filled with a sense of peace and purpose that once seemed impossible. The scars from my past, both physical and emotional, remain, but they no longer define me. Instead, they serve as reminders of my strength and resilience.

I've learned that happiness isn't about avoiding pain or challenges, but about finding the strength to overcome them. It's about appreciating the small joys, nurturing meaningful relationships, and continually striving for personal growth.

To anyone who might be facing their own struggles, I want to say: there is hope. No matter how dark things may seem, there is always a path forward. It may not be easy, and it may not be the path you initially envisioned, but it exists. Don't be afraid to reach out for help, to lean on your loved ones, and to believe in your own strength.

As I look to the future, I'm filled with optimism and excitement. I don't know what challenges or opportunities lie ahead, but I know that I'm equipped to face them. My journey has taught me that life is precious, that second chances are possible, and that with perseverance and support, we can overcome even the most daunting obstacles.

I'm grateful for every day, every breath, every moment of joy and even the moments of struggle. They all contribute to the tapestry of my life, a life that I once nearly threw away but now cherish deeply. As I continue on this path, I carry with me the lessons of my past, the love of my family, and the hope for a bright future. This is not the end of my story, but rather the beginning of a new chapter - one that I'm excited to write, one day at a time.

Dear Readers,

Thank you for journeying through The Worst Thing Ever Happened. As you close the final chapter, may you find strength in the shared stories of hardship and hope. Each page reflects the resilience of the human spirit, and we hope it inspires you to embrace your own challenges with courage. Remember, every ending is a new beginning, and there is always light to be found on the path ahead.

With gratitude and hope,

Jatin Bharat and
Respected Authors

CONTACT US

+91 730 792 80 40